We Walk the Way

+

Trace the sign of the cross on yourself slowly and deliberately.

They seized Jesus and led him away.
Peter was following at a distance. *Luke 22:54*

Sing to the tune of Stabat Mater:

Join we all that long line walki
Age to age we're singing, talking,
Crossing borders, time and space.

Join with pris'ners, soldiers, gawkers,
Mourners, children, fools and hawkers.
Lift the precious cross so high!

Who's to judge this wand'ring preacher:
Prophet, rebel, gentle teacher?
Arms and troops give Rome the pow'r.

The First Station

Jesus is condemned to death.

+

We adore you, O Christ, and we praise you,
(genuflect)

because by your holy cross you have redeemed the world.

So Pilate gave his verdict:
He handed Jesus over. *Luke 23:24, 25*

**Dying, you destroyed our death;
rising, you restored our life.
Lord Jesus, come in glory!**

Kneel. Pause. Pray.

Stand. Sing. To the next station:

**Dead man walking, takes so willing
Isaac-like, the wood of killing.
Cross, be strong and do not fail!**

THE SECOND STATION

JESUS ACCEPTS THE CROSS.

We adore you, O Christ, and we praise you,
(genuflect)

because by your holy cross you have redeemed the world.

Jesus, carrying the cross by himself, went out to what is called The Place of the Skull.

John 19:17

**Dying, you destroyed our death;
rising, you restored our life.
Lord Jesus, come in glory!**

Kneel. Pause. Pray.

Stand. Sing. To the next station:

**Child of earth, the earth embraces;
Bloodshed all God's work defaces.
Stones and soil, be cradle dear.**

The Third Station

Jesus falls for the first time.

+

We adore you, O Christ, and we praise you,
(genuflect)

because by your holy cross you have redeemed the world.

Are you the city that kills the prophets and stones those who are sent to it? *Matthew 23:37*

Dying, you destroyed our death;
rising, you restored our life.
Lord Jesus, come in glory!

Kneel. Pause. Pray.

Stand. Sing. To the next station:

She who sang God's table-turning,
Poor ones lifted, rich left yearning.
Knows this struggle through and through.

The Fourth Station

Jesus meets his sorrowing mother.

✝

We adore you, O Christ, and we praise you,
(genuflect)

because by your holy cross you have redeemed the world.

A sword will pierce your own soul too!
Luke 2:35

**Dying, you destroyed our death;
rising, you restored our life.
Lord Jesus, come in glory!**

Kneel. Pause. Pray.

Stand. Sing. To the next station:

**Come to me, your burdens bearing,
Take my yoke, made light in sharing.
Gentle, humble be your heart.**

The Fifth Station

Simon of Cyrene carries the cross for Jesus.

+

We adore you, O Christ, and we praise you,
(genuflect)

because by your holy cross you have redeemed the world.

They compelled a passer-by to carry Jesus' cross. *Mark 15:21*

Dying, you destroyed our death;
rising, you restored our life.
Lord Jesus, come in glory!

Kneel. Pause. Pray.

Stand. Sing. To the next station:

Lynching snarled by mercy tender:
Simple kindness, simply rendered.
Brave and good Veronica!

The Sixth Station

Veronica wipes the face of Jesus.

+

We adore you, O Christ, and we praise you,
(genuflect)

because by your holy cross you have redeemed the world.

When was it that we saw you hungry or thirsty or a stranger or naked or sick or in prison?
Matthew 25:44

Dying, you destroyed our death;
rising, you restored our life.
Lord Jesus, come in glory!

Kneel. Pause. Pray.

Stand. Sing. To the next station:

Love that made all time and matter,
Shepherd struck, the flock to scatter:
Weary flesh and weary earth.

THE SEVENTH STATION

JESUS FALLS A SECOND TIME.

We adore you, O Christ, and we praise you, *(genuflect)*

because by your holy cross you have redeemed the world.

He has borne our infirmities, carried our diseases. *Isaiah 53:4*

Dying, you destroyed our death;
rising, you restored our life.
Lord Jesus, come in glory!

Kneel. Pause. Pray.

Stand. Sing. To the next station:

Bethle'm's mothers, Rachel weeping,
Comfort banished, death's long reaping:
Till you women wake our God.

The Eighth Station

Jesus meets the women of Jerusalem.

+

We adore you, O Christ, and we praise you, *(genuflect)*

because by your holy cross you have redeemed the world.

Daughters of Jerusalem, do not weep for me,
but weep for yourselves and for your children.
Luke 23:28

Dying, you destroyed our death;
rising, you restored our life.
Lord Jesus, come in glory!

Kneel. Pause. Pray.

Stand. Sing. To the next station:

With the poor from all the ages,
Disappeared ground down, in cages:
On their backs the mighty ride.

The Ninth Station

Jesus falls a third time.

+

We adore you, O Christ, and we praise you,
(genuflect)

because by your holy cross you have redeemed the world.

My soul clings to the dust;
revive me according to your word.

Psalm 119:25

Dying, you destroyed our death;
rising, you restored our life.
Lord Jesus, come in glory!

Kneel. Pause. Pray.

Stand. Sing. To the next station:

Naked came I from the womb so;
Naked now to cross and tomb go:
My baptizing now at hand.

THE TENTH STATION

JESUS IS STRIPPED OF HIS CLOTHES.

+

We adore you, O Christ, and we praise you,
(genuflect)

because by your holy cross you have redeemed the world.

They divided his clothes among themselves by casting lots; then they sat down there and kept watch over him. *Matthew 27:35*

Dying, you destroyed our death;
rising, you restored our life.
Lord Jesus, come in glory!

Kneel. Pause. Pray.

Stand. Sing. To the next station:

Bend your boughs, Tree, low and lower.
To your breast now hold this lover:
Sweet the nails that pierce you through.

The Eleventh Station

Jesus is nailed to the cross.

We adore you, O Christ, and we praise you, *(genuflect)*

because by your holy cross you have redeemed the world.

They crucified him, and with him two others, one on either side, with Jesus between them.

John 19:18

Dying, you destroyed our death;
rising, you restored our life.
Lord Jesus, come in glory!

Kneel. Pause. Pray.

Stand. Sing. To the next station:

Death and life are here contending;
Christ has died, all hell upending:
God so loved this wayward world.

The Twelfth Station

Jesus dies on the cross.

+

We adore you, O Christ, and we praise you, *(genuflect)*

because by your holy cross you have redeemed the world.

Jesus gave a loud cry and breathed his last.
Mark 15:37

Father, I put my life in your hands.

Kneel. Pause. Pray.

Stand. Sing. To the next station:

Blood and water, Christ our brother,
Born with you we'll live for others:
Ever live beneath your cross.

The Thirteenth Station

The body of Jesus is taken down from the cross.

+

We adore you, O Christ, and we praise you,
(genuflect)

because by your holy cross you have redeemed the world.

They took the body of Jesus and wrapped it with the spices in linen clothes, according to the burial customs of the Jews. *John 19:40*

Dying, you destroyed our death;
rising, you restored our life.
Lord Jesus, come in glory!

Kneel. Pause. Pray.

Stand. Sing. To the next station:

On the seventh day God rested,
So when Christ by death was tested:
Sabbath sleep in new-made tomb.

The Fourteenth Station

The body of Jesus is laid in the tomb.

We adore you, O Christ, and we praise you, *(genuflect)*

because by your holy cross you have redeemed the world.

Joseph took the body and wrapped it in a clean linen cloth and laid it in his own new tomb, which he had hewn in the rock.

Matthew 27:59

Dying, you destroyed our death;
rising, you restored our life.
Lord Jesus, come in glory!

Kneel. Pause. Pray.

Stand. Sing. To the altar:

Come with fragrant myrrh, O Mary.
Cry: Arise, O Christ in glory;
You firstborn of all who die.

—

At the Empty Tomb

+

We adore you, O Christ, and we praise you,
(genuflect)

because by your holy cross you have redeemed the world.

You are looking for Jesus of Nazareth, who was crucified. He has been raised; he is not here. Go, tell his disciples that he is going ahead of you. *Mark 16:6*

Glory and praise to you, Lord Jesus Christ!

A homily may now be given.

Prayers of intercession are offered.

The Lord's Prayer is sung.

After the blessing, all depart in silence.